A Garden Alphabet

by Isabel Wilner
pictures by Ashley Wolff

DUTTON CHILDREN'S BOOKS   NEW YORK

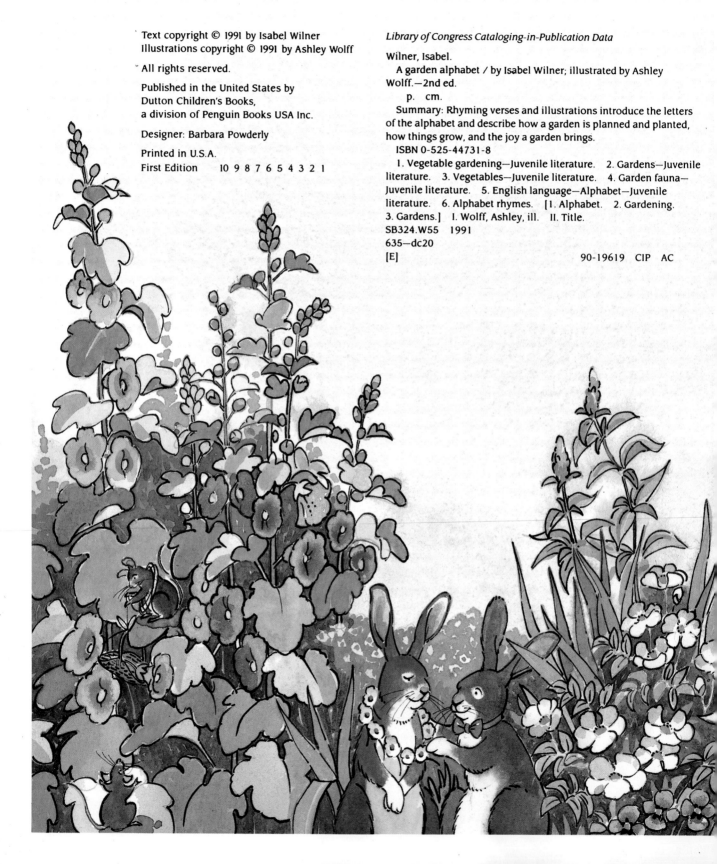

Published in the United States by
Dutton Children's Books,
a division of Penguin Books USA Inc.

Designer: Barbara Powderly

Printed in U.S.A.
First Edition   10 9 8 7 6 5 4 3 2 1

Library of Congress Cataloging-in-Publication Data

Wilner, Isabel.
   A garden alphabet / by Isabel Wilner; illustrated by Ashley
Wolff.—2nd ed.
      p. cm.
   Summary: Rhyming verses and illustrations introduce the letters
of the alphabet and describe how a garden is planned and planted,
how things grow, and the joy a garden brings.
   ISBN 0-525-44731-8
   1. Vegetable gardening—Juvenile literature.   2. Gardens—Juvenile
literature.   3. Vegetables—Juvenile literature.   4. Garden fauna—
Juvenile literature.   5. English language—Alphabet—Juvenile
literature.   6. Alphabet rhymes.   [1. Alphabet.   2. Gardening.
3. Gardens.]   I. Wolff, Ashley, ill.   II. Title.
SB324.W55   1991
635—dc20
[E]   90-19619   CIP   AC

For two gardening friends,
Ella Bramblett and Maud Broyles
—I.W.

For Pumpkin, of course
—A.W.

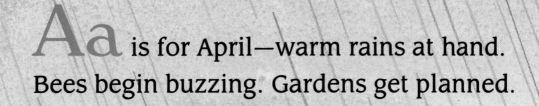

Aa is for April—warm rains at hand.
Bees begin buzzing. Gardens get planned.

Bb is for boundary, the edge of the plot.
Inside is garden. Outside is not.

Cc is for catalog,
a gardener's guide.
Some plants are favorites,
some not yet tried.

Dd is for dirt.
Down go the roots.
When a seed sprouts,
up come the shoots.

Ee is for earthworms.
They live where seeds sprout
And loosen the soil
as they burrow about.

Ff is for frog, a gardener's friend.
For unwelcome insects, his tongue snaps The End.

Gg is for grasshopper, a gardener's foe,
Eager to eat what's beginning to grow.

Hh is for hoe—
what the gardener needs
To turn over dirt and to
root out the weeds.

Ii is for inchworm
whose measuring walk
Marks the width of a leaf
and the length of a stalk.

Jj is for June—
warm days, sunny hours
When butterflies flutter by,
buttering flowers.

Kk is for kale, with leaves dark and wrinkled.
Its edges are crumpled, curly, and crinkled.

Ll is for lettuce, a leafy sphere molded—
Green layer upon layer, all carefully folded.

Mm is for munch—what the rabbits will do
If they find that you've left them a carrot or two.

Nn's for nasturtium,
a flower so bright,
Blazing red, orange, yellow—
like flashes of light.

Oo is for onion. When it's tender and small,
You can pull it right up and eat
bulb, stalk, and all.

P p is for peas resting plump in a line
In a little green hammock
that grows on a vine.

Qq is for questions. To pick? To let grow?
A book and a look and a gardener will know.

Rr

Rr is for rabbits, back here once more.
Do they think they're the ones that the garden is for?

Ss is for snail slipping over the loam,
Taking its time, taking its home.

Tt's for tomato—
ripe, juicy, and fat.
No garden can offer
better than that!

Uu's underground,
where some vegetables grow,
Like the beet, carrot, radish,
and the *poe-tay-toe*.

Vv is for vines.
Whether pumpkin or bean,
They're twisty and twiney
and leafy and green.

Ww's for water—
from can or from hose
Or sometimes from rain
that just comes and goes.

Xx is excitement.
No time to be wasting.
Whatever is ready
is ready for tasting.

Yy is for year,
with winter for sleeping,
Springtime for planting,
fall and summer for reaping.

Zz is for zzzzzzz.
Those are bees on the wing.
Alive in the hive, they'll be
back in the spring.

DO NOT
DISTURB
UNTIL SPRING